RED ROVER RED ROVER

ALSO BY BOB HICOK

Hold

Sex & Love &

Elegy Owed

Words for Empty and Words for Full

This Clumsy Living

Insomnia Diary

Animal Soul

Plus Shipping

The Legend of Light

BOB HICOK
RED ROVER RED ROVER

COPPER CANYON PRESS

PORT TOWNSEND, WASHINGTON

Cover art: Doug and Mike Starn, *Attracted to Light Film Still 1,* 1996–2003.

Copper Canyon Press is in residence at Fort Worden State Park in Port Townsend, Washington, under the auspices of Centrum. Centrum is a gathering place for artists and creative thinkers from around the world, students of all ages and backgrounds, and audiences seeking extraordinary cultural enrichment.

LIBRARY OF CONGRESS CATALOGING-IN-PUBLICATION DATA
Names: Hicok, Bob, 1960– author.
Title: Red rover red rover / Bob Hicok.
Description: Port Townsend, Washington : Copper Canyon Press, [2020] | Summary: "A collection of poems by Bob Hicok titled Red Rover Red Rover"—Provided by publisher.
Identifiers: LCCN 2020017909 | ISBN 9781556596117 (paperback)
Subjects: LCGFT: Poetry.
Classification: LCC PS3558.I28 R43 2020 | DDC 811/.54—dc23
LC record available at https://lccn.loc.gov/2020017909

98765432 FIRST PRINTING

COPPER CANYON PRESS
Post Office Box 271
Port Townsend, Washington 98368

www.coppercanyonpress.org

For Eve

CONTENTS

Listen

To un-
become or scream or drown or dread, to if, to crown
a wear of heads upon my thorns, to then and when and yes and please
and love, or how a spoon can shine and drive a moon insane,
explain: upon my breath I have no ice in mind, nor stab or beat
or leave an ant or ghost behind, to hold and braid and brace
and lift a face, a sigh, if dive is rise and lies a poor disguise.
A gift should kiss its horse upon the mouth: I troth to shrug
and run and dream and lash myself unto my past,
to walk as if my muddle is a map that looks to me
to lead it home, to sing an edge upon a steel that cuts a split
into a join, if one is math and hole is whole, if I am fall and fear
and skies, if you will stand before a door hewn into air and time,
and thrive, and knock, I will wear my heart upon my eyes

RED ROVER RED ROVER

A partial list of a life

A bird says *You are home, you are home* at the window.
I put down my suitcase and try to soothe the jet out of my ears
by saying hello to the bird and then nothing at the table
to the salt and pepper. Running my hand over the claw marks
where Sasha jumped on the table to empty the sugar bowl,
I decide five years is the half-life of my mourning
and begin planning maybe considering possibly thinking about
accidentally turning into the shelter in another five years,
though not necessarily getting out of the car to meet
the unwanted dogs. Ten feet away is an X on the floor
only Eve and I can see where Eve collapsed
when her brain tried to run away from itself
but was stuck in its panic room and clawed her frontal lobes
instead: luckily I was there to hold her and turn the fall
into a whisper instead of a crash. Here's where we light the menorah
every year, taking turns with the match. I was standing here
for "no cancer" and there for a different call
that made me wish I had a hook to pass through my nose
to remove my bones and set them free. Every time I pee
I stare through a big window at a mountain that fits inside
the window like a painting; through that door's a field
we've crossed naked with naked stars; down there's a river
we can see flash a bit depending on where we stand
and hear samba some when rain has tried to wipe the slate clean
of dirt and all of us. If these walls could talk they'd have mouths
and lips I'd be happy to kiss. A baritone wind
just pulled itself out of its own hat and I know a better poem
when I hear one: wind and crows, wind and crows, wind and robins
and the silences between them and crows.

For the sad Wallendas

If the sky set out to be beautiful
we'd turn away or throw our shoes at it
or call it pretentious as we went to sleep,
none of which has happened on my watch
except the second and those were flip-flops
and it wasn't the sky I was trying to hit
but whatever makes a friend stick a needle in his arm
as if sewing the rip in his blood closed. When he died
the logical response was *duh,* the emotional response
was louder, more smashy/breaky
and I see this in people all the time
when I'm looking in the mirror, out the window,
at a park, a car, to the end of Canned Goods
where a woman cries in the direction of a can of peas
and I almost touch her shoulder as I pass, with my hand
and also a deer, the spirit of leaping, then I'm off
to peaches and barely hanging on
to the trapeze of the day, you say falling
I say when, you say net
I say the great ones
go without, as well as the plain ones, the stones,
the feathers, the torches, and everyone in between

The feast

I'm hungry. Nothing I've put in my body
has changed this. I ripped Genesis from a bible
and devoured it, thinking I'd feel filled
and whole and walk up to deer and stars,
rest my forehead against theirs and telepathically
talk to them as equals, but they all ran away,
deer majestically and stars at a speed
I can't begin to comprehend. Do you worry
we've offended stars and they're abandoning us?
I do. And you. So on behalf of my anxieties,
I say sorry now on principle to you
and any trees or otters or planets
I have harmed, and look forward to the earth
turning me into sustenance. An aria comes to mind:
A poor woman must feed her dead husband
to their starving children. She's convinced
she'll go to Hell whether she does or doesn't.
The question she ponders in the aria:
Is the dilemma itself Hell
and has she been there her whole life?
It's an Italian opera so the cruelty
of poverty has a natural poetry to it.
They're almost the same words—*poverty* and *poetry*—
as are *dagger* and *danger, mangle* and *manage,*
lover and *lever, inspiration* and *kazoo.*
When her dead husband sings back to her,
he praises her skill as a cook and suggests
the loving ways she might prepare him
to give life, as she gave life so long ago.
I don't cry as much as I used to
and wonder if standing in the rain
would replenish what I seem unable to give,
visible proof that I long to be absorbed
but recognize that I can't be.

The life of the rough night

I found her in the morning cutting hair from her head
to burn or banish on the river,

a practice run at mourning. Why wait?
She'd risen from bed

to think about the dead getting closer to her parents
by the day, to not sleep

a little differently on the couch from how she'd turned
like a lathe on her side

of dreaming. She'd taken a crowbar to the dark, her eyes red
from trying to break inside

what has no end or center or beginning, while all night
crickets taunted,

Nothing changes. If you want to be reborn, die;
if you want to love,

hurry up: what's a year, a decade, a life to water: a person's
a sheaf of rain

in a thirsty world. Rain rain don't go away: there is
no other day.

Prepare for takeoff

We were poor.

My Mr. Potato Head was a potato.

My pony was half a red crayon that drew all of a red pony.

I rode my red crayon pony with my eyes closed.

Mr. Potato Head died slowly of mold.

The potato who replaced him was also from Idaho.

They'd traveled far to let my imagination put words in their lack of mouths.

Later, when I had money, I'd carry a hundred dollars in my underwear.

It seemed a fortune, and the idea of a fortune kept me warm.

When you're poor, you never stop being poor.

When you're a potato, you never stop smelling like dirt.

Scared of the dark, I'd hold the aroma of earth to my nose
and think of Mr. Potato Head in the night of the ground.

If he survived, so could I.

If people called the gross knobs that grew out of him eyes,
I was free to believe whatever I wanted.

This is how I learned to fly.

Postcard

Looking at a bird.
Looking at the moon.
Looking at a bird looking at the moon.
Sharing a cigarette with the trees
outside my hotel room.
Waiting for Pegasus.
Standing in my socks.
Finding a yellow knife in my coat pocket
that doesn't belong to me.
Stabbing a beer can.
Dropping the knife in the trash.
Wondering what kind of bird sings
for a man waiting for a horse that flies.
Wishing I'd taken more acid when I was young.
Imagining myself in armor in the pool
reading *The Unbearable Lightness of Being*
as children a thousand years from irony
competitively splash each other
for the prize of shouting *I Am the King.*
Never be the king,
I whisper from behind my faceplate.
Everything is happening at the same time.
You are here and I'm in your bedroom
looking at your slippers.
Why yellow? Why open-toe?
There are only surprises,
including how little I understand.
My head is on fire and I think
it's because I have a woodstove
for a soul when the truth is
fire has to be somewhere,
I have to be somewhere,
everywhere has to be somewhere:
why not here?

Refraction

In Alaska the sun had insomnia:
I chased a rainbow at midnight
south of nowhere in a rental car,
having lost my favorite cap.
As fast as I went, the rainbow went.
As awake as I was, the sky never blinked.
As much trouble as I have
being around people, Alaska agrees:
Alaska gives humans the cold shoulder,
the frozen river, the scary bear.
I love that Alaska wants to be alone, too.
For hours, the world was empty
of McDonald's, lawn mowers, For Sale signs,
capitalism; it was like looking in a mirror
that ignored my face, that saw
where I really came from, that stared back
at the savanna inside my bones.
I pulled over and built a house
of my affection: I would live there
with distance and mountains
and the intelligence of rainbows,
who are smart to be untouchable.
If we caught them, we'd put them in zoos,
cut them open, try to civilize them,
teach them French, teach them war.
I pulled over, sat on the hood
and leaned into the air
with my capless and bald head,
the bite of it, the hello of it,
and decided to stand taller within myself,
like a swing set or giraffe.
I've driven along fracked fields,
where mountains have been scalped
and refineries channel apocalypse

with their forests of pipes, their fire
and smoke,
and while some places make me eager
for lobotomy, Alaska
makes me want to be better, think better,
do better: to fit in. Not that I know
what that is or means. Not that we can.
Just that we better. Just that we must.

Inside job

He talks more than a river.
Louder than a gun
doing the times tables.
Sometimes he smells
like three-day-old scallops.
Sometimes four.
Whatever anyone says to him
is reason to say something
about himself.
I avoided him in the halls.
I avoided him as an idea
of what a person might be.
I once saw him up ahead of me
and turned around.
I was in New York,
he was in Boston.
That's how good my eyesight is.
That's how much he made me think,
Here is a man
who'd trim his toenails
in an airport.
Then I saw him in a park with a boy.
The boy was wearing a helmet.
The boy could barely stand on his own.
The boy's eyes always looked up
and his head bobbed
as if studying to be a balloon.
This is Trevor, the man said,
this is my son. The man smiled.
Though our faces are no good
at putting out forest fires,
his happiness could have,
his pride. This is my son.
He said it twice

as if I hadn't heard,
as if making sure
I would spread the news.
I will spread the news.
A man who smells
like three-day-old scallops
has a son named Trevor
who will never live on his own.
Now when I see the man
I ask after his health.
I want him to live forever.
I want the moon to stop
sneaking away from us
a little at a time.
I want him to forgive me
for giving up
on looking into his eyes.

A nature documentary

Worrying I worry too much,
I try to explain Jell-O to my cats,
who sniff it and walk away,
one to watch a wasp
digging out a hole under a rock beside the shed,
the other to watch the wasp-watching cat
while I eat Jell-O on the porch with my fingers.
Two at first, then my whole hand,
as if orange Jell-O were an actual orange,
not all of it,
just a few slurped chunks from the pan,
after which I join the watching of the wasp,
no longer worrying about worrying, just worrying
and enjoying the relative quiet,
like when the dentist's drill stops
and I can hear the chainsaw solo
without distraction in the orchestra
of my head.
Curious whether the sky is where I left it,
I lie on my back on the drive and look up;
it's still there,
though none of the paintings of clouds
are dry.
The white cat comes over quickly
and licks the hair on the side of my head,
as if I'm another cat. I turn my head,
look in his one milky and one green eye,
love that he's adopted me
and lick his head a few times to show it.
And for about seven seconds
I'm not even worrying, not even
about the cat hair in my mouth, thicker
and more honest than human hair,
the other cat on her way down the drive

to look for frogs to kill
and partially eat or not eat at all,
the white cat already at ease
with himself at all times,
when I start to worry again,
now that I don't know how lucky I am,
that there's no unit of measure for gratitude,
as the narrator says, *Once again we see the poet*
not leaving well enough alone,
starting a fire from water and stones,
when actually I can start a fire
from anything, even an avalanche,
especially a tornado, though most of all
nothing at all.

Yes this again

How goes prosecuting Nazis? The OGs,
not the new ones. I can ask a friend that
of his daughter. You probably can't
so I'll ask for you, too. It's a great world
that offers these little comforts
for its mistakes, that takes a degree from Harvard
and turns it into remembering lives
only photos[1] recall, not their details
but their worth. He's proud of her
and I'm proud of us. We could say, So what? And do
about so much. But not this: we agree genocide
needs to be snuffed out. Mostly.
Though studies show kids don't know
what Auschwitz is, was. That flies
are still easily separated from their wings.
That we are us. No amount of law or dreaming
changes that. Maybe some amount of love.

1. Grainy, fading, black & white: memory trying to forget itself.

A lament, pep talk, and challenge walk into a bar

Banjo. Zither. Carnegie Hall. The Four Tops and Seasons.
Greek chorus. Music of the spheres and triangles
and dodecahedrons. The Kinks. The Mozarts
and Fats Wallers and Puentes. The Butthole Surfers.
My office is bigger and more flexible than my heart
and this is a weird way to critique my affections
but so be it: the intervention is under way. Do you feel
small? I feel tiny lately. Like a good person
would remove the doors of his house and give the poor
a controlling interest in JPMorgan and storm congress
with onesies and pillows and hold that flotilla of egos
hostage in a sleepover until the Kindness Act is passed
unanimously and do unto others goes from words
dropped in the suggestion box to law. Why aspire
to the part of a thimble when galaxies
are shinier role models? I should be putting meals
on wheels or moving Miami to a higher elevation
or helping strangers with their calculus homework.
I speak shovel, yammer hammer, have drills and bits,
wrenches and jigs, elbows and frontal lobes, and have noticed
when I throw up my hands in frustration
they come back, that they take their responsibilities
to hold and carry seriously, and so should I
be a ladle or hammock, spoon or cradle, a yodel
or some other reaching across the distance
to the factions and splinter groups of the tribe
or clan of woman and man. It's no accident I began
this meandering with music: no two species
could come from more distant planets
than a Steinway and sax,
yet listen to how well they get along
when they put their mouths where our fears are,
when they lend us our better-tuned selves. My ears
were raised by Ray Charles and Johnny Cash, so I hum

and flow and stumble, rasp and trance and moan
between two sets of certainties, that we are angelic
junkies, fallen and blind, and that we can rise
and see. The deepest soundtrack of my being
is a black man and the Man in Black
breathing into me the one and only commandment:
Don't just have but be a soul.

Interlude

In the little swale where my wife sleeps
to my right, I grow roses
whenever she goes away
for the weekend to see her family.
A place for everything
and everything glowing
on the inside if you close your eyes
and look. How old will I be

when I die? Zero: a babe in the arms
of the afterlife. How old will I be
when I figure out how to stand
unobtrusively among the junipers
growing taller and more resilient
in the night? She comes home,

sees the roses and knows
I've been up all night
watering our life,
caretaker of the presence
of her absence. Hello
my deepest breath. Hello
falling through space
from our little while together
standing still.

Under construction

I meant to be taller,
I tell my tailor, who tells my teller,
who cashes my check all in ones
to suit the height of my ambition.
And kinder, I tell my trainer,
who trains my tailor and my teller too
to look better wetter and drier, kinder
to people and blue skies, moles
and Republicans, even though
it takes more muscles to smile
than tell someone to fuck off.
I ask my tuner to listen to my head
and tell me whether it sounds out of sorts;
she says a man's not a piano
and cries, for wouldn't that be nice,
a man you can sit in front of
and play like Satie turning a piano
into a river speaking to its mother,
the rain, late at night. But she's sweet,
my tuner, and tightens a few strings
in my back just to get the old tinka-tinka
up to snuff before she kisses me
on the cheek. Life. I think that's
what this is, the glow
where she smacked her lips to my skin,
birds acting surprised that the sun
has sought them out once again,
and me looking in my closet
in the morning and choosing
the suit of snails
over the suit of armor.
Who remind me to slow,
to savor, as if they know.

On having a month off

To have time to be yourself. To fall in love with beets.
To cook for shut-ins. To attend the bat mitzvah of a cloud.
To mourn the passing of fingerprints from a window.
Time and a cyclotron. Time and pinking shears.
To reach for a volume of Maupassant, fall off the ladder
but not hit the ground, to never hit the ground again.
To sit quietly in the birthing room of the morning.
To work on your theory that the night sky
is a bottle of champagne being opened.
To have a heart-to-heart with ennui and a Manhattan
and a way of bending light as it travels around your hips,
your sighs. Time and a pet scorpion. Time and a stack of paper,
envelopes, three pens and the address of every person
you've passed who was crying in their car
and no greater plan with them or the universe than to say,
"I see you, I saw you, I seesaw across my days, same as you."
To come to peace with this form of travel. To put your hand
on your mother's cheek from a thousand miles away.
Time and a deep breath. Time and time when time runs out
to look at me and see me carving my eyes to the shape
of your face. To get older, shorter, lighter. To fit
in a pocket. The little pocket that belongs to the pocket
of jeans. If you are you. If I am me. Folded. Held.
Somewhere. Someever. To make a wish and blow out
the conflagration. Ashes to ashes. Dust to blood.

Falling

Moonlight in bed with us. Our first ménage à trois.
The ménage à quatre must be 33 percent better.
Why doesn't everyone hump everyone at the same time?
I count everything. Number of halos on a coatrack.
Times I've thought cats have tiny rock tumblers
in their throats. To purr is to polish a velvet stone.
When I purr I sound like a river that smokes too much.
Smoking used to be sexy like the industrial revolution.
You can't French-kiss moonlight. You can put a rose
in its hair. A whole garden for that matter is excellent
courting. If night is a movie theater without sticky floors,
the moon is the star of the show. Stars are extras.
I must be the key grip or best boy. Best at what?
Cherishing the tiny crack in the glass bauble of my being?
Having the soul if not the shoes of a flaneur? Looking
a gift horse in the mouth? Know what I see? Teeth & tongue. Abyss.

Plans for the day

Pancakes. The men's final at Wimbledon.
Carrying around the phrase "Where I go I cannot follow"
as a tryout epitaph. Looking at, probably working on
the retaining wall above the culvert under the drive
that was just replaced. Wondering a hundred times
whether our cat is getting better or dying less obviously.
Taking the mountains for granted: taking the mountains
for granite: hating puns: loving the womb
one word is of another. Thinking in odd moments
of money. While brushing the teeth of our shark.
While watching a cardinal peck at its reflection
in a window. Do we have enough to retire
and look at koi ponds
as indulgences of people who need better hobbies?
Do we give enough to people in need?
Who is not a people in need?
Beginning a letter to America:
Dear richest country in the history of ever,
Please share. Struggling for the next sentence:
Share everything. Share now. Thinking of barn raisings
while wondering what our aversion to collective effort is
on a larger scale. Remembering all the times
I saw "WPA" on sidewalks in Ann Arbor and Detroit
and New York and felt warm in whatever part of me
loves people working together
to give others a stable path forward,
as they make their way
into the shine and tumult. Getting older.
I will get older today. Add a *b*: bolder today.
A *c*: colder today. Add a moon visible in the afternoon,
a ghost moon of the blazing moon to come
and maybe pizza and maybe looking at Eve
in the garden at dusk forgetting everything
but having hands amid the handless flowers

that are nonetheless five-petaled
in how they reach for the sun. Go figure. Go home.
Kiss your doorbell. Your thermos from childhood.
Your fear of the dark. Kiss everything:
some small percentage of dust
will kiss you back.

Family matters

I asked the sun if it had a favorite planet
but it saw through me (mostly with neutrinos)
and gave me the cold shoulder.
Realizing I'd displaced my curiosity
by ninety-three million miles,
I asked my parents which of their children
they love the most. To my surprise
my father said his lawn mower and my mother said
the child she miscarried in 1962, whom she loved
as much as the child she miscarried in 1963,
neither of whom I knew about and both of whom
I could see were buried in her eyes.
I went back to the sun and asked
why it had kept this from me. It burned and burned
and loved the hell out of every green thing
for miles, every leaf and blade reaching up for light
reaching down for them, a relationship
both public and private,
for I could see the result of the affection
though I'd never step inside it.
A month later my father told me
he loves his lawn mower
for going in smaller and smaller circles,
for letting him feel
as if he's solving the problem
of how to get to the center of something
while he worries about all of his children,
the dead ones, the living ones,
the ones he wanted to have
and the ones he would have had
if he and my mom could have kept up
with the example of the sun.

Buzz

August and I've not seen a single fly.
Are they dead or shy? One monarch
but no swallowtail butterflies. Two toads,
one hopping, one squished where the road
meanders as if it forgets where it's going,
or why. No bats or snakes—black rat, garter—
a few hawks, some wild turkeys the other day
in my yard, a few vultures but not enough
to cut circles in the sky. When I had hair,
bees and bugs were everywhere: fireflies
made Christmas trees of July. A kid born today
will think they blink in dozens; her child
will hear the myth of electric nights,
as I was told of passenger pigeons
that blacked the sky for days. August
and I've not shooed a single fly.
When life is being subtracted from life,
it takes a long time to notice
and longer to noodle that eventually
we'll be thinned or nixed and won't
be missed. August and if they'd come,
I'd be a man and not hurt a fly.

The description I carry in my wallet in case Eve goes missing and I go mute

Too peaceful to chew ice, too big for her bed
in the dream of her dollhouse,
too soft for a career in sandpaper,
too sad about her mother to curtsy
to the Champs-Élysées, too kind
to tell the sky it can be a real bastard,
too wet to be the out-of-body-experience
of rain, too expansive to be the thread
to anyone's needle, too tired to fold napkins
into swans, swans into ballerinas, ballerinas
into eating disorders, too shy to be a forest fire,
too introverted to be an orchid, too sad
about her grandmother's death
to trim a single branch from a single tree,
even a dead branch, even a branch that has fallen,
that has evolved to a stick, too honest
to be the best friend of a mirage,
too gentle to play the tambourine,
to make it as executive producer of *Star Search,*
to go out for drinks with a hostile takeover,
too sad about her grandmother's death
to die herself in case the dead
aren't allowed to miss the dead, too much like air
not to be breath, too green
not to be spring, too mortal
to be one of the floating women of Chagall
and too mortal not to be the appetite
of his colors for the sun, too elsewhere
when she is gone, too gone when I blink,
too much of a garden for me to carry
in my not enough pockets, mouths, hands

Good fortune

When he was seven, two memorable things happened
in a row. He saw a man run over a snake
with a mower, back up and run over it again.
Being the kind of kid to tattle,
he went inside to tell his mother.
He found her in her room, naked in bed,
about to switch on her vibrator. At the time,
he didn't know what that was.
She told him it was a special thermometer
only women use. She got dressed
and made him a bologna sandwich.
Cut the crusts off. Sliced it on an angle,
the way he liked it. He told her
about the man and the snake. She said
some people are afraid of snakes—maybe
he just wanted to make sure it was dead.
She also told him some people are cruel
all the time and some people are cruel
part of the time, like on Tuesdays and Thursdays.
The lie about the vibrator had pleased her.
He believed her totally. This was maybe
her favorite thing about being a mother.
That her words left her mouth, entered his head
and built a nest there from which sparrows
eventually flew. She went on to say
that some people have stilts
instead of bones and some people
grow apples from their arms and some people
can walk through walls, like his father,
who disappeared one day. She did not say
"up and disappeared," as most people
would have. The "up" part of that phrase
implied that all disappearances
begin from a seated position,

and she knew that wasn't the case.
He liked the reasons she gave him
for why his father wasn't there.
His favorite was "Some men
have this part on their body
they want to share with everyone
they can." He asked her
if he had that part too. "I don't think so,
honey, but it doesn't show up
until boys get older." He thought of it
as a little machine with gears
like the music box of his sister's
he took apart, only instead of playing
a song, it told you when the moon
was going to be full,
so you could be sure to look at it
from your bedroom window. The sandwich
was good. The snake went away
from his thoughts and came back,
went away and came back. When he asked
about the humming sound he heard
some nights, she told him
a happy house makes that sound
very often if you're lucky.
"Are we lucky," he asked.
"It sounds that way to me," she said.

No suicide is not an island

We were on different schedules.
As my failed attempt was putting me in the hospital,
she was learning from my mistake,
crossing out *Valium* in her head
and looking seriously at buying ludes
from Tony and stealing them from Jane.
The day I was released I went to her funeral
despite the rain's advice,
sat a hundred yards away behind an oak
to spare her parents thinking of killing me
and me thinking of offering her parents a gun
to put to my head. Boxes in the ground
is one of our few inspired ideas. I'm talking space,
not hygiene: imagine us stacked
like shoes, wing tips and pumps,
loafers; we'd run out of room for the sun.
Her note to me was the kind of thing
a piccolo would say to a drum: *Shhhh.*
I've taught my depression to tiptoe, whisper,
sit in the back of the movie
of my life, its head in the hands of the dark.
Hardly a day goes by
that I don't get out of bed, or mean to,
or wonder why I ever would.

Once more, from the top

Sex has changed for my wife and me as we get older.
The less of it contrasts with the better of it.
It's also simpler. Gone are the pulleys, orchestras,
moons. Sometimes we just look at each other in the kitchen
doing dishes or say *Zanzibar* simultaneously and have orgasms
or remember our best ones and shout those dates
at the spoons or whatever else looks like an ear.
I don't recall my first orgasm or my first time
down a slide or the first time I robbed a bank
or the first time today I realized I wasn't breathing
and took a series of deep breaths to catch up.
Let's bury *The Book of Why We're So Nervous*
up to its neck and pour honey over it
so ants will devour our problems and one
or more of us can get gluten-free pizza for the group
to celebrate our symbolic defeat
over our resemblance to insects in terms
of how crushable we are. I mean, if you want to.
My wife and I could also meet you for drinks
and not bring up the sex stuff or the crushing nature
of existence stuff, or even better, for bocce ball
with an old deaf Italian man who'll explain the game
by acting out the Thirty Years' War, as if life
is but a competition for space
when it's also a competition for clever desserts
and intimacy. Like right now, the me
who wants to write this poem about loving my wife
is fighting the me who wants to actually love my wife
by greeting her this morning as she wakes
as slowly as a sack of potatoes growing eyes.
That sounds mean but that's really how she wakes.
Which reminds me that *organic* is one of the few words
that sounds like *orgasmic,* which is one of the few words
I hate to say, like *moist* or *ouch* or *death,*

which reminds me that telling the truth is important
but my question has always been, Tell the truth what,
other than go away and leave us alone.

More than whispers, less than rumors

The river is high. I'd love to smoke pot
with the river. I'd love it if rain
sat at my table and told me what it's like
to lick Edith Piaf's grave. I go along thinking
I'm separate from trash day
and the weird hairdo my cat wakes up with,
but I am of the avalanche
as much as I am its tambourine.
The river is crashing against my sleep
like it took applause apart and put it back together
as a riot of wet mouths
adoring my ears, is over my head
when it explains string theory
and affection to me,
when it tells me to be the code breaker,
not the code. What does that mean?
Why does lyric poetry exist?
When will water open its mouth
and tell us how to be clouds, how to rise
and morph and die and flourish and be reborn
all at the same time, all without caring
if we have food in our teeth or teeth in our eyes
or hair in our soup or a piano in our pockets,
just play the damned tune. The river is bipolar
but has flushed its meds, I'm dead
but someone has to finish all the cheese
in the fridge, we're a failed species
if suction cups are important, if intelligence
isn't graded on a curve,
but if desperation counts, if thunderstorms
are the noise in our heads given a hall pass
and rivers swell because orchestras
aren't always there when we need them, well then,
I still don't know a thing.

On the rocks

I hate ice in whiskey, on my car, my nipples.
Ice is water that's too good to look me in the eyes.
Ice leads to hockey and hockey leads to Canadians
with gap-toothed smiles. What do we say of the dead:
cold as ice. But ice doesn't deserve to be killed.
First of all, it's fairly reclusive, mostly hangs out
at the poles. Without ice there'd be no polar bears,
arctic terns, penguins. Watching penguins swim
and not get eaten by orcas makes me happy.
Watching orcas eat penguins makes me believe the world
is a self-regulating system and I should mind my own business.
Was a self-regulating system and we did not mind
our own business. What is our business? What do we add
to the endeavor? Don't say cathedrals, Beethoven,
two-for-one sales on diapers and Colt 45s. Do say carbon dioxide,
heat, ignorance of our effect on whales, monarchs, winter.
What if the world is a grape and we are a bruise?
What if we're being given what we want most of all,
we who are the memory singers, nostalgia machines:
what if elegy is our calling and we need death
to feed our desire to lament how good things were
before cars, Jiffy Pop, Botox, Miracle-Gro,
us? We tell one story: Eden. Once upon a time
things were better. Once upon a time
our minds were simple and we were happy. Once upon a time
human nature wasn't what it really is
and that's all it took to live at ease in the garden:
to not be us.
If your nature's your danger, your gist a fist,
your essence a pestilence, what do you do
to not be you? Kill yourself or evolve. Sorry:
I meant to write an ode, a ditty about something wild
and pretty. That's how it is with us—we almost always
mean well: to give strangers a ride, eat more vegetables,

vacuum the house, not ruin the world. To be kind
and that fabled, mythic thing—wise.

Pedagogy

The red-haired green-eyed woman to my left is alone,
she tells me in a note, and tired of being the only lesbian
in this room. I look around. Of the thirteen other
possible lesbians, I rule out eleven based on purses
and shoes. I write this back to her and she agrees.
I'm the teacher so passing notes is fine
with the authorities. We're both bored
with the presentation on Charles Olson.
I seem to remember that "Projective Verse"
wasn't reprinted in a volume celebrating his work,
as if the editors recognized a fart disguised as an essay
when they smelled it. The presenter would have done better
to twirl flaming machetes. His voice sounds like a shoe
being drowned. She writes that the two possible lesbians
would make an attractive couple. I marry them
in Tahiti and get a little drunk on sunshine
in my thoughts. I don't know what to write to her:
that everyone is alone like a key to a safe in the safe
at the bottom of a well at the bottom of a sea?
Her solitude is not my solitude, which can wear
a live alligator on its head and still hide in the open.
I'm trying to get her to say what she says to me
in these notes in her poems, but a note
is the most private genre after the shopping list.
I finally suggest that she open a gay bar
in the northeast corner of the room. She asks
what to call it and I tell her I'm just an idea man,
execution is up to her. But I have no guillotine,
she writes back just as the student finishes
hurting me inadvertently with his passion.
The red-haired green-eyed woman is next. The note
she gives me as she stands confesses that she'd rather
eat a rat while it's shitting out the remains
of the smaller rat it ate than stand in front of people

who probably hate her. As she writes "Audre Lorde"
on the board, I write "Audre Lorde" in my notebook
and underline her name twice. I try to make the word
"theater" out of "hate her" but need another *t*
and one less *h*. I really want to read the poems
in which her solitude speaks to mine like two new kids
in first grade sharing potato chips on the edge
of a playground while throwing their carrots at a turtle.
We'll see what happens in this life and the next.
I don't know how to teach people a thing, I write on a note
I give myself. That's OK, I write back: what you lack
in intelligence you make up for with biting the inside
of your lip. I wish I believed him but he'll say anything
to suggest that everyone's running around with a parachute
on their back and a hand on the rip cord
so why not help each other find the escape hatch
or ground the plane due to the fog
we're in. As if life's as simple as levitation
or the perfect martini: eighteen parts gin
and three parts gin and gin and an olive orchard
and don't bother with a glass and gulp and gin.

Remedy

In deciding what I am, I've ruled out cat, vulture, shoe,
a sadist who tortures people to death in a Syrian hospital,
a president who separates families at the border,
a handful of purple irises at the beginning of the path
to heaven. Is there memory in the shade of a tree
of a lynching fifty years ago, when I was nine? And do I love
that tree? Love the sinner, not the sin. Forgive the electricity,
not the singeing of genitals. The more I know about human nature
the more I plan to be tall grass in a field. Until then
I'll tell my wife I love her in Toronto and Blacksburg and bed,
in pajamas and blue jeans and song, in theory and fact and dream.
I will not gouge a man's eye out I promise, yet the eye is out,
the man is dead, and the geese I'm listening to have no idea
that we're as wild as the coyotes that would tear them apart.
If given a choice I'd not choose to be human. If given a choice
how to be human, I'd say like a glass of water. While I have
no answers to the questions I don't know to ask, I can love my wife
in Detroit, in general, in detail, in vain, in spite, in depth,
in the shallow light of the moon, in contrast to hating myself,
in sympathy and in stealth, in time as a ghost and right now
as a poet wondering if surgeons, during a transplant,
tell the shivering and recycled heart it is loved. I assume so,
but I've never asked a heart on its second time around,
Were you christened, were you blessed, are you worth
all this trouble?

Silo City

A Nigerian poet and I are pinched together
at a corner of a table in a Buffalo bar
trying to hear each other. A three-piece band
is playing alt-indie-folk-rock: the amplified sincerity
hurts my spine. I've just read poems
in an abandoned grain silo about fifty yards from the bar.
After telling me where he was born and that he's a student
at Syracuse, he mentions a fellow student, a young poet
who'd been e-mailing me but stopped, adding, "Your work
meant a great deal to him and he killed himself,"
a sentence that pushes me out of the window of my head.
New to America, new to death, he found the body.
This is why his face has no moon or sun in it, no hawks
or clouds, nothing that rises or glows or flies. Mostly
he feels guilty. If he hadn't gone on a trip; if he'd paid
closer attention; if he were God. That last one is me.
We're aspiring to be a cave, our heads almost touching
as I shout that he couldn't have known something was wrong
and that suicides are often unplanned.
The most vivid way to convey this is to explain
that when I tried to kill myself, I had no intention
to do so: packing for a rafting trip,
I put a rolled-up T-shirt in a duffel, turned around,
walked into my parents' bedroom, grabbed several bottles
of Valium, left the house, drove to a field
and swallowed my sudden desire for erasure.
I'm screaming all of this against the sonic wall
of a song about the end of love. I can't tell
if he hears or understands me, if I hear
or understand me, even though I'm close enough
to see the complexity of his irises, the swirls
and privacies of their colors. My words are daisies
trying to stand up to a lawn mower. I sense that even
if he heard me it wouldn't matter: I'm pretty sure

he's ash, or sticks thrown against a wall,
or a Francis Bacon painting beaten up in an alley,
pretty sure I'd love to be a blanket or ladder
or a leaf that's always green against his heart.
While the impulse to help is stupid,
the impulse not to is a metal spoon
against a cavity. Now I feel guilty.
I haven't shouted loud enough or grabbed his face
and kissed the bruises out of his eyes
or chewed down to his brain and licked it,
haven't proven the value of language
to reach and assuage. Over and over the singer
has a broken heart. Is this all we do, try to connect
and fail? There's no way to keep this up:
the band's attempt to lasso tumult
is killing me, I have to go, I have a life
that isn't this, isn't Buffalo,
isn't his friend's decision to find out what happens
after pizza and blue water and not having the right words
for our jealousy of light. I don't even know his name
yet am convinced that I'm abandoning him
as I walk away, that this is a practice betrayal
for all the betrayals to come,
of flesh and the earth and that every time
I close my eyes, I kill the sky that lives there.
I decide I'll write him a poem that cures solitude
and send it to everyone but him; that I'll write
everyone else a poem that cures arrogance
and send it only to him; that I'll be ready
to find a body or be a body that is found.
I decide nothing. I walk out of the bar
and become the cool air that touches my skin.
I don't look back, or forward, or side to side.
I am air. I look everywhere, I look nowhere at once.

Weather report

It's snowing. December ninth
twenty seventeen. No tracks in the snow
on the deck, along the cedars, in my mind,
that combination jungle gym & jail cell.
I just watched a video of a starving polar bear.
It looked like brooms wearing a polar bear suit.
No Arctic ice. No ice means no seal hunting.
No seals means no living. It looked like a blanket
that had taught itself to walk. Let's talk
about something else. Do you miss cocaine?
Sometimes I do when it snows. It's the resemblance
of shivering to doing a line. I never did much.
Not enough to get a polar bear high. Maybe
a seal. What animal would you be if you could be
any animal that isn't endangered by climate change?
Is a roach an animal? A rock? Rocks
are in the clear, and roaches exist
in the popular imagination—the imagination
everyone wants to date, the imagination
that gets all the girls and boys
and ocelots—as the creature
that'll be eating our Twinkies
after apocalypse. Nothing
kills roaches and Twinkies
goes the thinking. No starving polar bears
to feel sorry for then. Let's talk
about anything else. When you were a kid,
did you wear Superman pajamas, or sense
it was ironic that you hid from the dark
by closing your eyes,
or think we'd break the world?

Hush little baby

After I'd shut everything off—computer,
computer, phone, TV, drill press,
fear of the dark—walked into a field
full of hay bales, sat down, closed my eyes
and tried to be exactly a man doing this,
specifically the tides of my breath,
the thought I couldn't let go of:
                          when does cut grass
become hay? When it's cut? Dried? When a horse bends,
eats, looks me in the eyes? I could have wondered
when does screaming become talking, when does drowning
belong on a résumé, can hummingbirds relax
without cigarettes? I could have grown old
and died. Instead I felt for the edge
of one thing becoming another
and found a smooth, untroubled surface,
just like when I tried to take a puddle apart
into rain or separate my time with you
from how surprised I am every morning
that the sun hasn't burned itself alive.

Genuflection

If a forest falls and no one is there
to catch it. If there is a last tree, last leaf.
If clear-cutting lacks clarity. If I am an accessory
to murder. If a conditional sentence
never finishes combing its hair. If a glacier dies
in Alaska. If a glacier is killed in Iceland
and buried at sea. If I like breathing.
If I like coral. If I like liking the blue Earth.
If forests had lawyers. If trees were CEOs.
If CEOs were angels. If an angel falls from heaven,
comes to dinner, opens her chest, opens his mouth
and stars pour out. If heaven rises. If heaven prizes
canopy, understory, overgrowth. If appetite. If covet.
If capitalism is suicide by comfort. If shrug.
If "Will you look at the time." If I abet extinction.
If I am an accomplice to *poof.* If trees are green engines,
god of every heart and lung. If clear-cutting
is our brains proving they're knock-knock jokes.
If who's there. If too late. If a tree is planted.
If a forest is guarded by the Secret Service.
If another tree is planted. If a forest stars
in the next superhero movie and the sequel
and the prequel and ta-da. If breathe. If you.
If Eden. If grace. If the apple is the word *apple.*
If a species falls and no one is there to notice
it is us. If I take a knee. If I die before I pray
to wake. If I pray we wake before we die.

Amsterdam: murmuration

Your shadow is born anew every time you step into the day or turn a light on or fall under the sway of the moon.

Your shadow is born true every time you fall into the day or persuade a light on or dream under the sway of the moon.

Your shadow is raised from the dead every time you erase the sun or can't escape the insomnia of the moon.

When I pressed the orange button below the speaker in the Stedelijk Museum, a woman who called herself The Composer read through this progression and kept going, the sentences morphing and compressing until she ended with this:

You are a generous kleptomaniac. You are a friendless lecher. You are a timid gravedigger. You are a flightless bird. You are ash.

While she spoke, on a screen above the orange button, a rat snake was run over by a car on a loop, or what seemed a loop, until I realized that ever so slowly, the snake avoided the car and moved on, was followed through grass all the way to a tree, which the snake climbed and then the screen went blank. Next, there was a not-quite-silence, an almost hush with an undertone of what seemed like breathing. Slowly it became clear it was the panting of a dog coming closer to the microphone, until it was licking it. This was followed by real silence, a silence that seemed eight miles deep due to the noise that birthed it. A silence that ended when someone—I think a man—started crying, slowly and softly at first, then faster and harder, repeating the word *light* the whole time through sobs and whimpers. After this, silence again, which was interrupted by The Composer saying, *The last silence had the shape of not crying, while the previous silence I call Absence of Dog.* Yet a third silence arrived, after which a child said, *You have pressed the orange button and asked it to be an oracle. The orange button has done its best. Now run away and be larger than you were before.*

The next day, I talked my former wife into coming with me to the museum. I said she needed to experience the orange button, though really I wanted to have a life with her any way I could. But when she pressed the orange button, it was completely different: while a video played of thousands of starlings changing direction, rolling and twisting their way across what felt like a breathing sky, the child who'd told me to run away the day before, repeated the phrase, *Art is the belief you don't need a tree to climb a tree.* When she pressed the orange button again, this came up on the screen: Only one astonishment per customer.

After that, we had coffee on the roof. I told her what happened when I pressed the orange button. The piece was called *Prophecy* and we both were in love with it, which I believed meant we were in love with each other, so I was shocked when she stood in the midst of me thinking I couldn't live without her and kissed my face goodbye, softly, as if taking a glove off and setting it on a river.

I keep making the mistake of approaching solitude alone

My wife and I were on our way to say goodbye
to a woman's ashes when a podcast
about a deaf guy came on her iPad. Podcasts
have taken over the role of novelists
as the keepers of narrative. A deaf guy.
Once-deaf guy. Sort-of-deaf guy. Who was moving
when he said, *"Don't Worry About a Thing"*
is a good theme when you're headed
into brain surgery. Pleasing Bob Marley.
Making an inadvertent pun—headed
into brain surgery. Once he knew his hearing
was going, he listened obsessively
to his favorite songs in an attempt to carry them
to the island of deafness. We say no man
is an island to protect the reputation
of islands. He lost his hearing
but got some of it back when a device
was implanted in his brain stem. His wife
was part of the podcast, too. She gave up medical school
to take care of him. They had a bunch of children
and sang Beatles songs to their kids
in the crib. *Moving* is a word I like.
It suggests levers and rivers and elevators
and jump shots and new locations
for the otherwise stuck heart. The heart
can't move and the woman's ashes
are not the woman. The body in all its forms
(flesh, smoke, dance crazes)
is never up to the task of identity.
We had cried in front of the ashes
when they were still a body. *Moving* is also
a word I mistrust, as narrative surprise
distracts us from the inevitability
of the plot of breath. The ashes

were and are my wife's grandmother,
and never were. In telling his story,
the man was trying to prove
he had listened to himself, whereas ashes
are horrible listeners. Without narrative,
the internal life is a performance
for a captive audience, yet the artist
often prefers the internal life to bodies
in all their forms (fog, crying daughters,
concealed weapons). I watched people sing
and read poems and cry and never felt
what they felt, I felt what I thought they felt
and pretended the two were the same.
This is the air I can't swim across. Why
is there only a stethoscope for blood?
I am an archipelago at best.
I'd have more faith in love
if we ate our dead.

My Tao

PROLOGUE

It's too hot for a blanket over my lap
but my dying cat won't jump up
if it's not there. A little bit of a breeze
through the window as I pet her head
and try once again to get more out of the Tao
open in front of my keyboard. Of the three versions
I have, I prefer Stephen Mitchell's incarnation,
as I prefer his Rilke to all others.
She's purring. I touch her between sentences
as I have while writing almost every poem
in this book. Mitchell: "The Master does his job
and then stops." I am no Master and I have
many jobs. Pet this cat. Write this poem.
Tell this breeze thank you. Remember Greece.
Change a mind in pieces to peace of mind.
Interpret that which cannot be interpreted:
a cat: a breeze: a book: a life.

1

The Tao that can be whispered
is not the eternal Tao.
The name that can be named
is not the eternal Phyllis.

The unnameable is the eternally real
and the easily lost.
Naming is the origin
of the label gun.

Free from desire, you confuse yourself
with a tree.
Caught in desire, you see only the manifestations
of not being a tree.

Yet *mystery* and *manifestations*
both begin with *m*.
This source is called alliteration.

Alliteration in the heart
is called a pulse.
The heart is a closet
within the closet of the body.
Existence has so many places
for coats and tennis rackets.
Few closets have lights.
To interrogate the darkness,
close your eyes.

2

Whoever relies on the Tao in governing
doesn't try to force issues
or make people listen to country music.
For every force there is counterforce.
For every apple there is a pie.
Violence, even when well intentioned
and well dressed, always rebounds upon itself.
Hence the broken knuckle, nuclear fallout.

The master does his job, stops,
gets a beer, reads from *The Arcades Project*.
He understands that the universe
is forever out of control.
That's not true: he understands
that his head is not the kind of flower
the universe wants to tell its secrets to.

Because he believes in himself,
he doesn't try to convince others.
Because he is content with himself,
he doesn't need others' approval.
Because he ordered a cheeseburger,
he also ordered fries.
Because he accepts himself;
because he is trying to accept himself;
because one day he hopes to accept himself;
because he has never lost sight of himself
as he danced, he worries his soul
is a guitar without hands.

3

It's good to be like water.
First, you are mostly water anyway.
You are related to making flowers grow
and solving thirst. Second,
water bends without yoga pants.
Third, water and gravity are lovers.
It flows through any crack
in any wall and pools in every low spot
in any driveway. The Tao says,
Think of yourself as a lake
on which you are also a sailboat
that gives no thought to the lake.
Thinking that way is also water.
Living that way is a deep breath.

4

The Tao is like a well: deep
but maybe not deep enough.
Producing but in danger
of running dry.

Expensive to drill
so get three quotes.
It is like the eternal void:
maybe, I don't know.
Sometimes I get too conceptual.
Sometimes I wish words
had thorns on them,
making what I say bloodier, earned.

The Tao is hidden
but always somewhere
around here, under the couch,
stuck between your chakras.
I don't know
who gave birth to it
or why the mind
can't conceive of origin
from nothing, but it can't.
Not really.
People say they can
but plenty of people
like tyrants too.

How old is the Tao?
Older than God? Is God
older than God?
No one knows,
but Happy Birthday anyway.
The Tao is eternally
an excuse for cake.

5

When you see her face as beautiful,
her knee becomes ugly.
When you see his work with the homeless as good,
your appreciation of his love

for commedia dell'arte
suffers in comparison.

Being and nonbeing are mothers to each other.
Difficult and easy cheer each other on.
Long and short hair define each other.
Before and after are different sides of
What time is it?

Therefore the Master
wears a watch on her watch
and acts the part of Cordelia
without rehearsing and teaches
without saying anything about the syllabus.
Things arise and she lets them come;
glasses fall and she gets a broom.
She has but doesn't possess
until the last house payment clears.
When her work is done, she goes home
unless she's working at home,
in which case she's already in her pajamas.

6

Because the Master doesn't take too much soup,
he doesn't spill it getting to the table
and embarrass his bowl.
Because she doesn't get so good at the Watusi
that the dance floor clears
and makes her a hermit of her motions,
she never dances alone.
Because she doesn't ask people if her wings
make her a Chagall,
she is quietly a painting by a Jewish mystic.
Because he doesn't stop himself crying
or not crying about a dying cat,
you will find him crying

while rinsing a blue cup
and not crying while wondering
if fog is a kind of mind.

Just eat and dance and fly
and sleep honestly after.
Serenity isn't looking for advice.

7

The Tao doesn't take sides:
red rover red rover,
send good or evil over.
The Master doesn't take sides:
she bets on both red and black.

The Tao is like a bellows:
it is empty yet infinitely capable
of being a device few people use.
The more you use it,
the more you're probably a farrier.
The more you talk of it,
the more you're probably talking
to other farriers.

Hold on to this job,
you seem to like farriers.

8

The Tao is called the Great Mother:
empty yet inexhaustibly stretch-marked,
it gives birth to children who later wonder,
Shouldn't I have had a say in this?

It is always present within you,
the voice saying, I'm doing a load of darks,

give me your darks.
You can use it any way you want,
just call home from time to time.

9

The Tao is infinite, eternal.
That seems redundant.
If something is eternal,
it is infinite in time.
If something is infinite, calendars,
even those cute nature calendars
with pictures of young bear
and fox on them, are beside the point.

What is the point?
The Tao was never born,
therefore it can never die.
It's half vampire, half God.
It has no desire for itself,
leaving more desires for you.

The Master is detached from all things
that don't have handles.
Because she has let go of self-interest,
her hands are free to hold your child
as you struggle to load the car at Target.
Half-off sale. Good for you.

It's not that the Master has mastered anything:
her troubles are the size of the sun.
She just knows not to stare at the sun.

10

You are the ventriloquist,
dummy. Hand up your own

(my) back, voice in your own
(my) head. What you say (think)
of God is not what God thinks (says)
of you. Too much to unravel
for your wooden tongue (hands).
There is alive (breath)
and alive (I have eaten
light), which is to say (feel)
that the whispers of being
are the ghosts of its thrive.
The opposite of speech
is river, not quiet.
How is it you sit in
your own (my) lap and speak
your own (my) thoughts
without either of our mouths
(souls) moving the moon (God)
to reply (sigh)?

11

If you overesteem great men,
stop it. Please.
Their egos bloom like roses.
If you overvalue possessions,
people rip your shit off
and sell it on eBay.

The Master leads
by emptying people's minds
of the idea of the Master.
He helps people
find the missing slide
for the Davidson project.
He fills people
with coffee or tea

or apple juice
if that's what they like.
Personally he prefers lemonade.

Practice not criticizing
other people's drinks
or sexual partners
or love for the *Duino Elegies*
in the dark.

Practice not doing
jumping jacks in elevators
and press 7, please.

I'll try to practice
being less bossy.

We'll get there,
wherever *there* is.

12

The Master says goodbye with advice:

Sit on the edge of the sky,
a roof, the mouth of a whale.
Look up and down and in.
Vanish all the steps
that have led you here.
You were not born.
You have never had toast.
Museums and all they believe in
have been folded and folded
smaller than the vocabulary
of a pocket. It's not
that you can unlist them,
tick off their unbeing

and say, Here is the shadow
of this and that,
of Enrico Caruso
and loving how my wife says
grape: a plain word
for a miracle. It is
that all the friendships
between sound and object
and memory are over,
all the handles removed
that make a tree a tree
and not a puzzledream,
and you are alone
with nothing but knowing
you are alone,
and of course my advice
to you: jump.

On the one hand

Almost instantly
she turned into an ax, her expression
I mean could have cut down a tree
and I wanted to go back to neutral,
to being someone saying,
I don't think you turned in your paper
to someone replying *I think I did*
and tried to get there
by smiling like a sock puppet
but it was no use,
her face was felling trees
and I realized I was pregnant
with a tornado, she was mad at me
because she thought I was mad at her,
which made me mad, which she could feel,
which made her angrier and I worry

this is who we really are
in a century intent on Armageddon,
this rain forest gone and that hurricane
dawdling over Barbados
as if putting on makeup in a mirror,
that we're slightly more rational
than weeds and barely more restrained
than jackals and less essential
in the scheme of chlorophyll and pulses
than ants or bees, and even when I made clear

there was nothing to worry about,
that whatever had happened,
she could give me the paper next class
and it wouldn't hurt her grade, she left
without saying a word and I spent
a few hours wanting to live alone

in a cave, and we are the creatures
who'll fix the aching world?

On the other hand

A child stands in front of a building holding a sign.
The child holds the sign, not the building.
The building holds politicians. She is fifteen.
The child, not the building. The building
is one hundred thirteen. Neoclassical
with Baroque Revival elements. The child
has unzipped-hoodie and braided-hair elements.
Her sign reads "Skolstrejk för klimatet."
I think you can translate that if you speak English
like this poem.
It's half as tall and twice as wide as she is.
The sign, not the poem.
I'm guessing six feet square, six feet hip: I say that
because she's the coolest thing on Earth today.
She's fifteen and skipping school
to stand in front of the Swedish parliament
and save the world. This makes her a role model.
This makes her President of Doing the Right Thing.
"School strike for the climate." I translated anyway.
I want to make sure I'm as clear as a forest fire,
as the hottest summer in 262 years.
She is Greta Thunberg.
She suggests the future has a future.
The future always has a past
but not always a future. She's fifteen and saying
stop flying to Paris, stop feeding oil to cows,
stop eating cheeseburgers by the barrel,
stop beating up the air and water and trees. She's saying
we know the future is committing suicide in our arms.
She's saying I'm doing this
because you adults are shitting on my future.
This poem doesn't know how to translate "shit" into Swedish.
The word, not the object. The object speaks for itself.
The metaphor speaks for us all.

We are shitting on breath, on species, on Dancer and Prancer
and butterflies and cats and cat videos and the blue-and-green marble
of Earth. This child is the oldest person in the room
of the world. She got the idea for the strike
from American kids skipping school
to say *No* to guns. They got the idea
from what the hell are we doing?
Kids are taking over. The future is saying,
"I am ready to do my job. I will shine,
I will have years to go in the days to come,
I will have eons up my sleeve, I will survive on a diet
of people not shooting themselves in the head,
the foot, the heart. No more guns
of horrible ideas. People will look up
and allow the sun to give them light, the wind
to fill the sails of their blenders and TVs,
they will face death and use it to cure the virus
of greed." I take it as a sign
that a child stands in front of a building
holding a sign. Of things to come. Of the rose in the soul.
Of the stars in our minds. Sometimes standing alone
is standing together. Sometimes kids
need to shake their parents awake
when they're drooling on the couch.
Sometimes it's too late for the future to wait
for the past to catch up.
There's a new action hero:
We Have to Do Something Girl.
She's faster than a moth
I'm guessing, stronger than my niece
perhaps, and has the superpowers
of wearing plaid shirts while holding a sign,
refusing to fly until she grows wings,
convincing her parents to turn vegan,
telling the UN to wake the hell up, accepting urgency
as her lord and savior,

of not being jaded while also being afraid to die,
of asking if we have a conscience,
if rational thought has been a hoax.
Look at us answering no, maybe, we don't know.
Look at the time. Look at the time.
Will you look at the time.

The thing is

A hummingbird visited my head, looked for nectar
in my ears, my thoughts, I wanted to be a rose of Sharon
in the best way, with roots that go a mile down
and talk to other roots of other people who are trees,
for bees to accidentally fly bits of my sex away
and the moon to look at me shyly all night.

The opposite of running with scissors
is sitting still as deer eat my grass and a bird
lands on my ear for all of the rest of my life, technically
some fraction of a second, more than enough time
for the Big Bang to occur or to change my mind
about getting into the car and driving
into an abutment I've had my eye on.

If I die before I wake
to the possibility that I am vegetable
as much as animal, that I may bloom,
know that I meant to clean my room first,
that of all my time struggling to fit in
to my old pants and being human, it wasn't worth it
and can I do it again?

Here, now, gone

We're standing in the road
looking at a dead fawn. His truck facing town,
mine headed toward home. It appears to be sleeping
on the double yellow, curled as if in tall grass
or on a down comforter in a video someone has posted
on YouTube about her pet deer. No sign of collision
or gunshot, garroting, heart attack: nothing but spots,
cuteness. The name on his door means he works
on the natural gas pipeline that'll run
from West Virginia to North Carolina.
The company that pays him has a reputation for ruin
worse than syphilis. Employees have been told
to stay away from locals. They stick to a hotel
near the freeway with a decor I'd call modern roach,
drink there, hone boredom, look at stars.
We both crouch to make sure the fawn is dead.
What the fuck, he says, staring at the desert
of my face, where there's no rain or hope,
only cactus, as I search the dry lake-bed of his.
He looks back at the fawn, brings his hands together
as if waiting for a Communion host,
makes a scooping motion with his hands,
then slides his eyes to the side of the road:
I'm being asked to help save a dead fawn
from the bonus carnage of traffic, the shredding
that suggests life isn't just delicate
but deserves to be erased.
We are the briefest couple
joined by common cause, move the fawn
and stand temporarily as men who have respected loss
for sentimental reasons. Then nod, become ghosts
in a moment we are the custodians of, holders
of the unholdable, wind telling the story of itself
to itself.

Long-distance call

Afraid of clowns, buttons,
including the word *buttons*. Of waking at four
the rest of my life, sweating for reasons
the night won't tell me. Of becoming a pariah,
or piranha. That I talk with people
about as well as gnats
perform a bris. That my only friend
will turn out to be a fallen oak
that continues to grow leaves.
That nurses and bankers and plutocrats
are laughing at me, that my paranoia
has no authority for wiretaps.
That my face makes strangers
turn to fascism. That my voice
is the comedy of piccolos
tuning up. That I mistake worry
for love, the creases in my forehead
for my arms around my wife, the moon.
That I am being eaten by the mirrors
of the self, one angled slightly
from the other, my narcissism
getting tinier and tinier
as my glass incarnations
run away from my flesh. That rain
will never tell me its secret. That dust
won't mention me in its autobiography.
That stones are geniuses
for having just the one big idea
their whole lives, the rest
is cheese, confetti, dread.
That I'll never train the monkeys of my thoughts
to stop throwing their shit.
That no one thinks of me and smiles,

thinks of me and sings, if only
by rustling their wings. Afraid

that I am what cancer would get, I woke up today
desperate to tell the truth: I need you
to save me, to nod at the other end of this poem
if you'd give everything you own
for one clear moment as one clear note
from a robin or clarinet, even the sound
of a man ripping the air as he falls
from wherever I am falling, and you, also falling,
hoping once to be beautiful, simple, precise:
can we hold each other on the way down,
one dragging of fingers across a chalkboard
in the arms of another? If such an anatomy

sounds familiar, you have my condolences,
my understanding, my love.

Having our cake and being eaten by it, too

How long can you say no
to crème brûlée and peanut butter cups, air-conditioning,
flying to San Fran, flying to New York, the big bag of Fritos,
a new iPhone, new toupee, new hair color,
remodeling the kitchen, a nose job, bigger boobs,
smaller bigger boobs when you get tired
of your bigger bigger boobs, two flat-screens
in the basement, air-conditioning, caramel corn,
sour cream on your baked potato with butter, the V-8,
the turbo V-8, the twin overhead cam turbo V-8,
masturbation, a third Coke, a thirty-second Coke, a line of coke,
a second loan on your house, building a plastic-straw factory
in Chicago, in Kuala Lampur, masturbation, the extra-large pizza
with donut-crusted crust, watering your grass,
cutting your grass, fertilizing your grass,
playing nine holes of golf, eighteen, the dream
of an air-conditioned golf course, air-conditioning:

I hate air-conditioning, resist it until July, late June,
until I sweat at night and can't sleep, until I'm tired,
until the ease of pressing a button three times
and changing the setting on the thermostat from OFF to COOL
takes all of what—a quarter-pound of pressure, two seconds,
the teamwork of a few million neurons—until convenience
kicks the ass of knowledge, until the future recedes
into the future, until I'm human, pass the Coke, the coke,
the Fritos, the next-day delivery of toilet paper, dog food,
and day-old bread: have you ever had pizza

while you masturbate, ever golfed eighteen holes on a plane
to Manitoba, ever told yourself, No, I won't eat that last piece
of chocolate cake, told yourself at six, seven, eight, nine,
ten, eleven, then got up at midnight, walked in dark
through a house your hands have memorized, flicked on a light,

snagged a plate, a fork, gently placed the cake on the plate,
walked it to the table, pulled the chair out, sat down,
and looked at love, your love of cake and your love of your life,
this air-conditioned and heated life that gives you cake,
and devoured the cake and your happiness and any chance
that you can say *No* when you need to, when we need to:

and of course now all I want is everything I want when I want it
plus chocolate cake

No you go

It surprises me how rarely

looking at a plane
I see anyone waving,

sitting on a grave
I hear a knock,

drowning at sea
I get thirsty,

dying for love
I pick up the phone,
my arms, the Garden
of Eden,
and love first.

Report from the field

The cricket inventory is going well.
A lot, a lot, a lot. The river's set list
rarely changes. I bought this land to be naked
in the later, saggier portion of my life
and not offend any cedars. The ground shakes
and vibrates: rocks bubble up
to ruin mower blades and be sat on
by crows. I've shot two wounded deer
in the head. After the third,
the deer make you an honorary bastard.
It says something about me
that I like watching cows eat
while they piss, maybe that I'm a connoisseur
of the waterfall, however yellow
or born, or that it's better
that I don't come to your house
for dinner. Thank you, though, for asking.
We'll see if there's a soul
or any of the superheroes are real
in the end. Spider-Man, Wonder Woman,
Captain Lava (if Captain Lava didn't exist,
we'd have to invent her). I love the imagination
for its garage bands and confetti
and continuing to shout, *You're not alone.*
I've got your back, your front, your sides,
your innards and outards, I've got time
to be immortal. Which is cool, since I don't.

Career day

Were I a stenographer,
I'd write down everything
rain says. A camper, I'd set up a tent
in the Rothko Room at the Phillips.
A heroin addict, I'd live in the '90s.
Jesus, I'd change it
to the Last Brunch. Quiche lorraine,
mimosas. I'd not take
a police psychologist's job
for anything in the world, other than
the world. And why do we say,
Shot his brains out,
when there's just the one? Were I a priest,
I'd only do straight weddings
and gay weddings together, couples lined up
down the aisle and around the block.
Let there be happiness and love
in bulk. Were I a star, I'd shine
binary. Were I smart,
I'd have been Jane Goodall
and kept my mouth shut. Why tell humans
apes are great when humans
are terrible at leaving apes
and well enough alone. But I am
dust, and as such,
I'll eat an apple
and be happy to give my shovel
a treasure map and beg the two of them
to dig the world. Were I a pun, hun,
I wouldn't be that one. Were I the Big Bang,
I'd whisper in the ears of flowers,
Take your time, this was all for you.

Kriah

Loss conflates without thought of scale
or decorum: eleven Jews shot dead in a temple
in Pittsburgh; songbirds pushed up a mountain
by rising temperatures in Peru
until there's nowhere to go, an escalator
of extinction; trick-or-treating
forbidden in a neighborhood in town
where the only danger is fear of the dark;
a cow shot in the eye across from our mailbox
because a motorist had a gun that could;
two people shot in the head in a Kroger
for being black; a season of dull leaves
falling, junkyard oranges and reds;
growing difficulty retrieving my name
from memory; tiny bits of plastic
in everyone's feces; tiny fits of crying
as I walk through the dairy section. Yesterday
I saw roses walking away from a hothouse.
Heard clarinets singing goodbye.
Watched my house write a suicide note
and begin striking matches. Today
someone told me about a Jew
who wasn't killed in Pittsburgh
or the concentration camp he was sent to
as a child. Who was late
for service and warned not to go inside.
Who should have been gassed, hanged, shot,
bayoneted, had his head smashed
against a wall, been driven over
by a truck, a car, history, been impaled
on a fork, on lust, been eaten
by lice, inmates, rain, snow, or just
thrown from the edge of the world,
but is alive right now in Pittsburgh

and getting ready for a funeral today. And instead
of pinning a piece of cloth to his chest,
is ripping the pocket of a favorite suit,
I hope, hard and fast, so a wound hangs
from his standing, his walking, his shadow,
the tatter of a flapping tongue
that belongs to his heart, that tells you
a beast has clawed at this life, and devoured,
and failed to kill the sun.

Zoom

No man is an island
but some women
are isthmuses
and many children
archipelagoes as they walk
in a wrist-roped chain
to the playground
so no one's lost
or stolen and everyone
finds their way
to being older
and wondering
what happened
to their mittens

Looking in the mirror

When I saw the headline
"Amazon is burning," I thought of the bookseller—
hawker of foot creams and radial tires,
bass boats, toothpicks, and avarice—
until I noticed the picture of rain forest
looking like a smoker's lung and realized my mistake
was loving cheeseburgers. Brazil is clearing land
for cattle. Cows are everywhere,
including a hundred yards from here
munching and meditating their way across grass
in the dark. If a tree falls in a forest
and there's no me there to hear it
because I'm at Five Guys ordering a cheeseburger
with mayo, ketchup, lettuce, tomato, and raw onions,
do you spell *culpable* with one or two
billion other people doing roughly the same? Sure
I'm just one person and you're just one person
but that's two just persons and you see the trend.
Remember the Inverse Square Law of Cheeseburgers
from physics: the further you get
from ordering a cheeseburger with mayo, ketchup,
lettuce, tomato, and raw onions at Five Guys,
the closer we are to being able to breathe
tomorrow and more importantly the day after
the day after the day after
the ten thousand years after that.

Love love me do

My wife's such a good person
she'd be an excellent dolphin
or whale. She eats kale, wears
Doc Martens, is smart enough
not to come out of the rain,
how else explain how green
her thumb and mind and smile
are, not that I need to
do more than accede
to my desire to surround her
with the sound of me saying,
"Is that an apple pie
in my pocket or am I lucky
I flunked suicide
at nineteen and zombied
my way to meeting you
eleven years later?"
That's a long sentence,
thirty years to life
if I hadn't happened
upon what is still, all sags
aside, the face
with the most upside
whenever I happen
to see her as if
I never have before. You know
how that is: you look up
from washing yellow eggs
off a red plate and being
sure your life's over
when there's your lover
or husband or wife
watching you with eyes
that could melt a cat, not

that you'd want to do that,
and you're what:
simultaneously torn
into confetti and reborn.
How's that for sticking
a thumb in the eye
of physics?

After you, or what would Whitman, Emerson, or Merwin do?

It's not too late
to schlep water in a bucket to your sink.
Eat only the potatoes and carrots
you can grow. Make your own clothes
from hemp and clouds. Go no farther
in a day than you can walk
or convince a river to carry you
on its back. Hunt wild chickens
or tame bear for dinner. Fall down,
break your leg, and set it between
two branches of oak yourself.
Accept the clock of the sun.
Turn a candle and the shadows
of your hands into TV, the story
of a haunted moon into TV,
sitting quietly before the debate
of crickets into TV. A little plowing,
digging, rooting for grubs,
spinning cloth, tanning hides,
felling trees, scything, midwifing,
burying your own dead
never hurt anyone
more than a lot, so let's go.
I'll send my 4Runner
to finishing school if you write
a Dear John letter to oil:
Not to be crude
but the hell with you.
On the count of three, never use
electricity again. One, two,
two, two, two

Stops and starts

Drove the night. As I knocked,
she was at my door, knocking.
Drove the day back to her note
and thought of her holding mine.
The phone rang. Did you see it, she asked.
I said yes, sure she meant the dead dog
we both passed, but she meant the spirit
of the dog trying to cross the road.
As soon as she said she stopped
and tried to touch it,
I saw a field of sunflowers
and wondered why I've never pulled over
and walked loose among them,
all those heavy heads nodding
toward my own. Weird that yellow's
the color of cowardice
when the sun never runs.
We fell asleep on the phone.
As blind dates go,
it was a good omen that we were happy
together alone.

I keep a weather station in my head

Lots of wet snow. The cedars are bent over
like a tall green woman looking down a well.
I worry the cedars will break under the weight.
I take a big stick and knock the snow off.
The cedars stand up like a tall green woman
hearing a goat screaming up in the hills.
I like goats. They strike me as self-sufficient.
I've never seen one at Home Depot
or coming into therapy with a hanky in its hoof.
The cedars are standing tall and the sun
is showing them how. I know my property
like the back of my hand knows I ignore it
unless there's a problem like when a cat bit me
and there is no well. My heart wants a well
or is a well or both could be true.
If you drop a stone into your heart
and it keeps falling, I'd see a specialist,
a theoretical physicist could tell you
when longing began to be a word
and not just what the universe is made of.
Would you believe I wrote this whole poem
in snow? Of course not. We're a civilized people
and no bladder is that interested in the arts.
Just parts of it, like when I wrote
I heard a cedar crack and crossed it out,
and wrote *I heard my brain crack* and underlined it
and crossed it out, and wrote *No snow globe
is this pretty,* which finally explained
the shaking feeling I've had my whole life,
ever since I stood up and gravity implied
it would let me get away with that for now.

Every machine has its parts

My father can talk to him but that's about it—
a guy you could sit beside in a bar and never know
he's picturing the knife in his boot
in your throat because you remind him
people exist and make noise—he is what war does
to some, a twitch covered in skin—a jester
should follow him with a song of warning
for the citizens or a doctor come before him
and inject small doses of Vietnam
into the eyes of everyone he meets—whatever's
easier—I prefer the needle
into our seeing what we ask soldiers to do—
certainly for presidents and senators a foxhole
should be required—some bleeding—a bit
of brain in their coffee—but I'm a poet,
you can excuse anything I say as antithetical
to reason—let me end then on a pleasantly
aesthetic note—my uncle can't hold a job
or conversation but carves robins and cardinals
that look so much like the real thing
I expect them to fly—one after another
and shoots them for practice instead of you or me

America: a primer

I sleep with a lot of women,
a lot of men, but my bed's

as big as my house, my house
is as big as the city, the city's

as big as the country, you see
where this is going?—

heaven's everywhere
someone needs a place to rest

and someone else says, Come in.

The Book of The Way: a song of now

September 27. Within thirty seconds of waking
I put on a T-shirt and pj bottoms made in factories
and shipped to me. Then turn on my laptop.
A computer equals more factories, shipping. Awake
less than a minute, I'm already drawing from the grid.
Even if I switch to solar, there's the plant
that'd make the cells and the ships and trucks
that'd deliver the cells to me,
the tools required for installation
born in their own factories and delivered
on their own ships and trucks. Then I make coffee;
beans from Ecuador packaged in Mexico; more factories,
shipping; eat a rice cake; a factory for the rice cake
and another for the bag in which it came,
plus shipping; feed my cat from a can; more factories,
shipping. Up ten minutes, I've been embedded
the whole time in an economy based on the principle
of maximizing self-interest. Nothing I've touched
was made by me or anyone I've sat next to on a bus
or kissed in a doorway or wanted to kiss
on the moon, and as the sun comes up I realize
I haven't seen a cardinal since July.

First do no harm to cardinals. First breathe
and let breathe. First admit we are wrongly named:
Homo insapiens. My enemies are not demons
but human beings like myself. First make a space
capable of innocence. First battle the genocide
of human desire. Do my arms need to reach
around the world? First do no harm to cuttlefish.
The life that can be made comfortable
is not the eternal life. What is too cold? Too slow?
Too demanding of my time? Should I make soap
and/or accept dirt as an equal? Should I grow wheat

and love it into bread? Should I bury my credit cards
and encourage rust to adore my car? Enter the battle
gravely, with sorrow and great compassion,
knowing I'm fighting human nature. First do no harm
to the sky. First accept smallness and be small.
Unplug one adapter. Unplug one heart from the dream
of more. Walk to buy milk, to Tahiti. Practice not-doing
and not-wanting. Whoever is stiff and inflexible
is an apostle of death. Whoever is soft and yielding
has the soul of water. First be rain. First flow.
Free from desire, what would I look like? Does my hand
need to lose its thumb? Has the mirror killed us?
Are we drowning in our reflections? If we un-nature
our nature, are we something else? Homo mutatus. First evolve.

When illness is cure

Moonmen gush over the blue: all noticed Earth
looked more alive and tenuous, more startling
and alone than could have been guessed.
On TV last week, one of them got stuck
repeating *fragile,* as if the word's gentle alarm
would wake us. After he spoke, shots of fires
and floods. When they returned to his face,
he seemed older, sadder: I imagined him
in the capsule reaching back,
putting a hand under the world
as if supporting the head of a child.
Comfort is the cause of climate change.
That we can create it to a degree
rats and giraffes can't. Comfort and ease.
Fridge of beer in the basement
to save walking upstairs.
Taking the car to get the paper
at the bottom of a long driveway
when it's raining. Clicking pictures of desires
until they abracadabra into our hands.
And pain will be the thing that saves us.
When New York becomes Atlantis. When only angels
are allowed to fly. When we have to shoot
our cars in the head. Push has to come to shove
for us: we're quick to notice
when the kitchen's on fire but not
when our way of life is burning down.
It's our nature: how many explorers
did the dishes, painted the living room:
the point was to leave home, not take care of it.
It's easier to ask what's out there
than in here, but the new moonshot's
internal: can we discover we love life

enough to save it from ourselves?
I won't be here to find out is why I ask.

O my pa-pa

Our fathers have formed a poetry workshop.
They sit in a circle of disappointment over our fastballs
and wives. We thought they didn't read our stuff,
whole anthologies of poems that begin, My father never,
or those that end, And he was silent as a carp,
or those with middles which, if you think
of the right side as a sketch, look like a paunch
of beer and worry, but secretly, with flashlights
in the woods, they've read every word and noticed
that our nine happy poems have balloons and sex
and giraffes inside, but not one dad waving hello
from the top of a hill at dusk. Theirs
is the revenge school of poetry, with titles such as
"My Yellow-Sheet Lad" and "Given Your Mother's Taste
for Vodka, I'm Pretty Sure You're Not Mine."
They're not trying to make the poems better
so much as sharper or louder, more like a fishhook
or electrocution, as a group
they overcome their individual senilities,
their complete distaste for language, how cloying
it is, how like tears it can be, and remember
every mention of their long hours at the office
or how tired they were when they came home,
when they were dragged through the door
by their shadows. I don't know why it's so hard
to write a simple and kind poem to my father, who worked,
not like a dog, dogs sleep most of the day in a ball
of wanting to chase something, but like a man, a man
with seven kids and a house to feed, whose absence
was his presence, his present, the Cheerios,
the PF Flyers, who taught me things about trees,
that they're the most intricate version of standing up,
who built a grandfather clock with me so I would know
that time is a constructed thing, a passing, ticking fancy.

A bomb. A bomb that'll go off soon for him, for me,
and I notice in our fathers' poems a reciprocal dwelling
on absence, that they wonder why we disappeared
as soon as we got our licenses, why we wanted
the rocket cars, as if running away from them
to kiss girls who looked like mirrors of our mothers
wasn't fast enough, and it turns out they did
start to say something, to form the words *hey*
or *stay,* but we'd turned into a door full of sun,
into the burning leave, and were gone
before it came to them that it was all right
to shout, that they should have knocked us down
with a hand on our shoulders, that they too are mystified
by the distance men need in their love.

Meditation on dust

No rain in months.
Mistings, spritzings, but no rain.
A trickle from our tap.
Grass is brown, dustbowl-ish.
I expect to see Tom Joad
with his thumb out for Cali.
Crickets have been breaking into our house
for the shade and vodka.
The era of clearheaded skies:
one blue thought all day,
one dark wish all night.
I'm considering having an affair
with a dowsing rod. I'm considering this
a spiritual quest: Jesus having visions
in the desert. A woman named Sally
having visions in the desert.
The guy who makes art out of tin cans
the same. I've always wanted visions.
Not always. Not when I was two.
Not when I was a trout in my mother.
But now that I'm a trout on my own,
I want a vision: my soul leaves me
and becomes a book of matches in the hand
of a bored and pyro-expressive kid
behind a hotel in Rochester, Michigan,
striking one of me after another
and throwing me at the air,
hoping to see existence catch
and light up in a manner befitting
the expectation that the body is a seed
chalicing an inexhaustible shine.
I also love the image of two people
leaning together to light a cigarette
in a hurricane, the little house of their hands

sheltering the preposterous flicker
as the storm plays its drum kit
against their spines. Haven't you had Tuesdays
like that, lovers like that, empty checkbooks
like that, isn't that the essence of waking up
every day and putting on underwear
and having coffee and knowing there's no manual
or compass or street-smart kid
coming to whisper the ways of the world
to your ear? If I don't die
of actual thirst, I'll die
of metaphorical thirst
or a car crash or old age. See?
Life is full of options and death
is full of nothing but the question
of faith: do you believe
in more less
or more more, in silence
that is silent or silence
that speaks? No rain in months
yet as the world unrivers, I hear flood.

Rapture

A woman wearing a waterfall, full length,
plays beautifully within and around the notes
required by the score.

Stops and stands within the quiet
born from the egg of that beauty,
a quiet that says nothing
in the manner of a crow
on a wire saying nothing.

Her dress falling and falling over her body.

Not a shuffle or ripple from the audience.

We have holstered our weapons.

We are holding hands.

We are remembering being zygotes.

We are breathing for our dead mothers.

When she exits stage left, the piano follows like a dog.

Of course it is breathing, of course music wags.

We follow the piano
like people tired of individuation
who want to be part of something bigger
than insomnia and debt.

At the bar,
everyone drinks whatever the piano is having,
everyone leans on their elbows
like the woman whose body is loved by a river,
everyone thinks the chandelier's a bit much

until we realize it's the Milky Way asking,
Am I pretty,
do you remember me?

When the bartender says,
You need to take this out-of-body experience
someplace else, we follow the woman
and piano home, tuck them into bed,
get in with them and dissolve
into how wired she is, how fused to our listening
she has become.

I write to you from inside a fugue state.

I write to you from the diary my shadow keeps
under its tongue.

I write to you from trusting the band of everything
will get back together.

I write to you from a wheeled chair on an angled floor
that keeps sliding to the west.

Sixteen years and I haven't fixed that.

Sixty years and I still want to be swallowed whole
by anything that will have me, a whale
or music or the way some skies look at me
as if we went to Livonia Stevenson together
or dated or stood on the Golden Gate
thinking about jumping into water on its way
to being bigger water, not to die but finally live.

Ode to now

We are squawking, walking, going mad,
going under, undergoing surgery, perjury,
losting and finding, minding our mannerisms
but not the store. We are stalking, hawking,
balking at engaging the mess we have made,
wounds to civility and trees, holes in sky
and soul, too busy, queasy, sensibly in love
with easy ways out or in or through,
depending on the day or door. We: me and you:
we two and we thousand million: we one
and all: how corral tens or billions or even
a few? And to or for what: love?
Of each other, kind, green? How sappy.
I'd be happy for quiet. This place shakes,
vibrates, is coming apart at the seams
as it seems we're afraid to do the most basic thing
we were born to: talk. As in sit and, as in can we,
as in I'd love to have a coffee or gin
or two thousand with you, here and now
or there and then, on Earth as it is in Heaven,
our daily gift of gab and bread, the reachings
of head to head. A word I adore
is *adore,* I guess *breath* most of all,
the grab and hold and lift and luck of it,
the chance we won't waste our chance
to be more like rain, to flow and shine,
touch and give as we wake up and go.

Worship

I stand under this tree missing Prince.
That tree missing Robert Frank. The sun touching me
between the two missings, doubling who I am,
a man taking inventory and a shadow
planning its escape. I love the sun. No half measures.
No *Sure, I can explode some hydrogen*
and send light ninety-three million miles
to your face if you insist. Imagine the sun
needing meth to leave the house. Imagine Marie Curie
on stage singing "Purple Rain." Imagine Prince
discovering radium. Imagine you don't know
what animates any living thing. I know a kid
who wants to be the Muslim Robert Frank.
I gave him an SLR for his neck. He gave me photos
of a man wearing nothing but a trash bag and a woman
kneeling beside an open driver's-side door.
I stand next to his face and think it a shrine.
I miss Stephen Hawking, and Jesus, my cousin Ruth,
Roberto Clemente and Ali and the days
I am dead, I miss being in the service of atoms
and the whispers that hold them together.
I stand under this tree wanting to be everything.
That tree trying to be the dot under an exclamation mark.
I never met Eleanor Roosevelt or the 1940s
but miss them and would jump at the chance
to jump for any reason. Like right now
crows are going apeshit and I just said that
and isn't it amazing that you know what I mean.
My wife will wake soon and I'll tell her the story
of clouds gone by and she'll tell me if she dreamed
and if she dreamed what she dreamed and we'll go on
being here as long as we can. Would you get in a plane
with Amelia Earhart? Yes you would. You're brave.

You have breath, which means you have terror.
Despite that, what will you do today? Eat. Look up.
Make the most of being the remains of a star.

Acknowledgments

Many thanks, hosannas, and hallelujahs to the editors of the following publications for including some of these poems in your pages: Academy of American Poets Poem-a-Day, *The American Poetry Review, The Common, Conduit, Diode, The Georgia Review, The Gettysburg Review, Kenyon Review, The New Yorker, Poetry, The Southern Review, upstreet, Verse Daily,* and *Waxwing.*

About the Author

Bob Hicok's ninth collection, *Hold,* was published by Copper Canyon Press in 2019. A two-time finalist for the National Book Critics Circle Award and recipient of the Bobbitt Prize from the Library of Congress, he's also been awarded a Guggenheim Fellowship, two National Endowment for the Arts Fellowships, and eight Pushcart Prizes. His poems have been selected for inclusion in nine volumes of *The Best American Poetry.* He teaches at Virginia Tech.

Poetry is vital to language and living. Since 1972, Copper Canyon Press has published extraordinary poetry from around the world to engage the imaginations and intellects of readers, writers, booksellers, librarians, teachers, students, and donors.

WE ARE GRATEFUL FOR THE MAJOR SUPPORT PROVIDED BY:

THE PAUL G. ALLEN
FAMILY FOUNDATION

 amazon *literary partnership*

 4 CULTURE

 the **point** envision·enact·evolve

Lannan

 ART WORKS. | **National Endowment for the Arts** arts.gov

 A& OFFICE OF ARTS & CULTURE SEATTLE

 WASHINGTON STATE ARTS COMMISSION

TO LEARN MORE ABOUT UNDERWRITING
COPPER CANYON PRESS TITLES,
PLEASE CALL 360-385-4925 EXT. 103

WE ARE GRATEFUL FOR THE MAJOR SUPPORT PROVIDED BY:

Anonymous

Jill Baker and Jeffrey Bishop

Anne and Geoffrey Barker

Donna and Matthew Bellew

Will Blythe

John Branch

Diana Broze

John R. Cahill

The Beatrice R. and Joseph A. Coleman Foundation

The Currie Family Fund

Laurie and Oskar Eustis

Austin Evans

Saramel Evans

Mimi Gardner Gates

Linda Fay Gerrard

Gull Industries Inc. on behalf of William True

The Trust of Warren A. Gummow

Carolyn and Robert Hedin

Bruce Kahn

Phil Kovacevich and Eric Wechsler

Lakeside Industries Inc. on behalf of Jeanne Marie Lee

Maureen Lee and Mark Busto

Peter Lewis and Johnna Turiano

Ellie Mathews and Carl Youngmann as The North Press

Hank and Liesel Meijer

Jack Nicholson

Gregg Orr

Petunia Charitable Fund and adviser Elizabeth Hebert

Gay Phinny

Suzanne Rapp and Mark Hamilton

Adam and Lynn Rauch

Emily and Dan Raymond

Jill and Bill Ruckelshaus

Cynthia Sears

Kim and Jeff Seely

Joan F. Woods

Barbara and Charles Wright

Caleb Young as C. Young Creative

The dedicated interns and faithful volunteers of Copper Canyon Press

The Chinese character for poetry is made up of two parts:
"word" and "temple." It also serves as pressmark for
Copper Canyon Press.

The poems are set in Minion.
Book design and composition by Phil Kovacevich.